# WellWriting

## For Health
## After Trauma and Abuse

Five WellWriting Ways to Regain
Your Health and Life

Ellen Taliaferro, MD, FACEP

D1729239

Creekside Communications
Half Moon Bay, California

Creekside Communications
Half Moon Bay, California

www.healthaftertrauma.com

| | |
|---|---|
| Editor | Ann Wright |
| | www.creekcom.com |
| Cover Designer | Stephanie O'Shaughnessy |
| | www.stephanieo.net |
| Publishing Advisor | Ann Walker |

## Warning—Disclaimer

This book is designed to provide information and to encourage improved health, functioning, and well-being through the use of expressive writing. The instructions and examples in the book are for your personal, private, informational, and educational use only. In no way does the information provided in this book replace, contradict, or diminish professional help from physicians and other healthcare clinicians. If you have questions about your health, consult a professional, qualified healthcare provider. The author and Creekside Communications will have neither liability nor responsibility to any person or entity with respect to any loss or damage caused, or alleged to have been caused, directly or indirectly, by the information furnished in this book.

# In This Book

# Acknowledgments

The author thanks so many who offered support and encouragement during the process of putting this book together.

For being great colleagues, readers, and reviewers, many thanks to: Liz Kinsworthy, MC, RN, CS, Administration of Resources and Choices, Domestic Violence Community/Heath Care Educator, Tucson, Arizona; and Diana Cummings, NP, Clinical Coordinator of the Keller Center for Family Violence Intervention, San Mateo, California

Special thanks to the founders of our Writers to Authors group: Pamela Armstrong, Ann Wright, and Jeanette Fisher.

When the student is ready, the teacher appears: Thank you teachers for becoming guides and a force in my writing life:

> Dan Poynter
> Sam Horn and her wonderful faculty at
> Cancun U:
>
>> Bud Garner
>> Mathew Holt
>> Stephanie Palmer
>> Cathleen Rountree
>> Christopher Vogler

Last, life is about learning, loving, and leaving a legacy. Thank you, OCW faculty and sisters, for telling me I could do all three. It's a long way from Chickasha, Oklahoma, and college days, but the lessons and friendship last a lifetime.

# About the Author

Dr. Ellen Taliaferro is a graduate of the University of
Oklahoma School of Medicine and a former Professor of
Surgery, Division of Emergency Medicine, at the University of
Texas Southwestern Medical Center. Dr. Taliaferro is a Fellow
of the American College of Emergency Physicians.

The author invites you to visit her website at
http://www.healthaftertrauma.com.

# Victim to Victor

**In 1999, a Chicago bus driver** shuttled busload after busload from the airport to the Hyatt hotel where a huge convention on domestic violence was headquartered. Our van was filled with people and chatter. Before we pulled away from the curb, the driver turned around and asked how many of us were going to "the big domestic violence conference."

Every hand went up. She nodded and began to drive to the hotel. A few minutes later, she announced: "I used to be one of those women."

The driver paused and fixed us in her gaze through the rearview mirror. Then she continued, "But I got out. I *was* a victim, but now I am a *victor.*"

At the time of the conference, I was an emergency physician. I had founded and directed the Parkland Hospital Violence Intervention and Prevention (VIP) Center in Dallas, Texas. Our VIP Center was the first hospital-based, medically directed center dedicated exclusively to caring for victims of violence.

At least 85 to 90 percent of our patients were victims of domestic violence. Many of them came to the hospital because they had been physically injured. Still others were referred to us from local shelters and domestic violence agencies for a "well woman" examination or other healthcare needs. We saw our mission as helping domestic violence victims become safe.

After the conference was over, I went home a changed person. Inspired by this brave bus driver who shared her history with us, I now realized that our job was not over until we helped the victims we saw become *victors*.

That is the purpose of this book. If you are a survivor of domestic violence or a supporter of a domestic violence survivor, this book will give you Five Ways to become a victor.

## About this book and you

Do you sometimes feel thankful that you have escaped the past abuse in your life, yet now you find yourself strangely stuck in life? Do you feel that you have more health problems than your friends who were never in an abusive situation? And somehow, you just can't get your life back together? Is so, or if you are a supporter of a domestic violence survivor who struggles with health and life challenges, this book is for you. It will show you simple Ways that you can follow to transform your life from being stuck as a survivor to thriving as a victor.

In this chapter you will learn:

- The toll that abuse and trauma takes on your health and functioning
- What's in a *Way*
- The stages of coping with abuse and trauma
- What's in your transformation toolkit
- The need to take charge of your journey

# The steps you need in your quest to become a victor

At the very beginning, let's establish two basic facts:

- It is *not your fault* that you became a victim of domestic violence and now suffer with the aftermath of the trauma and abuse that you sustained. It is in your hands, however, to overcome the disastrous results of that aftermath.

- Life is not about what happens to you, *but what you do with what happens.* You can suffer — or, like the brave bus driver, you can overcome your suffering to become a victor. No one but you can do this for yourself.

Abuse and trauma take a toll on your health and that toll prevents you from functioning at your full potential. Survivors of abuse and trauma often suffer from various chronic pain conditions:

- Increased anxiety and nervousness
- Insomnia, depression, and panic attacks
- Stress disorders ranging from mild to the severe form of post-traumatic stress disorder (PTSD)

In addition, some survivors experience suicidal thoughts or severe self-neglect.

# Become a victor

In spite of the toll of victimization that you experienced, you, too, can become a victor. You can achieve a state of better health and at the same time reach for and achieve your full potential.

The bus driver who gave us the "victim to victor" insight told us that she had won over her circumstances. She declared herself a winner and announced her success. She was a winner because she succeeded, and she succeeded because she learned to master her own life and circumstances.

# What's in a "Way"

 A quick trip to the dictionary will show you that the word *way* has several different meanings. A *way* can be a trail, a route, a certain distance, a characteristic and regular manner of being, a description of progress, or a condition or state.

A way can even be a spiritual path as noted in book titles such as *Way of the Peaceful Warrior, 20th Anniversary Edition: A Book That Changes Lives* or *The Artist's Way: A Spiritual Path to Higher Creativity.*

The Five Ways in this book present you with skills, tips, exercises and suggestions that will help you to master your own life and circumstances as you seek to master becoming a victor.

Victors have several things in common:

- They define their own unique gifts and determine to succeed using those gifts and talents to the best of their ability.

- They learn to master the nay-sayers that take up residence in their minds
- They learn to overcome their fears and doubts.
- They become enlightened to the fact that the purpose of life is to love, learn, and leave their own unique legacies.
- They learn to be persistent and to love themselves as well as those around them.
- They don't deny their anger—they find it, express it, and use its energy as rocket fuel to aim for the moon.

# Suffering sets the stage for transformation

When you transcend your current obstacles, sufferings, and distress, you become a stronger and more viable *you*. Life is about loving and learning. As you move toward becoming a victor, you will learn how to love yourself and overcome the suffering and distress in your life.

Victors often say, "I would never have chosen for this to happen to me. Still I know now, that I am better off than before because now I am stronger and wiser."

# Stages of the journey

Having had the privilege to work with and know many survivors of domestic violence, I now think of domestic violence as progressing through four stages. Leaving and recovering from domestic violence is not an overnight event, but a process that is a journey.

## The victim stage

If you are still in an abusive relationship or trying to extricate yourself from one, *this book is not for you.* Your job right now is to become safe, which often becomes a full-time endeavor. Once your safety is guaranteed, then you are no longer a victim but a *survivor* of domestic violence. But going from one who survives to one who thrives is another challenge. Leaving is a huge undertaking.

If you need help right now, call the National Domestic Violence Hotline to find local resources:

# 1-800-799-SAFE

**If you are in immediate danger, call 911 or go to the nearest emergency department, fire station, or police station.**

## The back-and-forth stage: victim-to-survivor-to-victim

As you may already have learned or experienced, many women who leave domestic violence relationships return to their abuser, not once but several times. Often they return for the same reasons they didn't leave to begin with.

Eventually, if the violence continues, they do leave, but it may take several efforts of leaving, returning, and leaving before the leaving is complete and final.

## The survivor stage

At this point, a former victim of domestic violence is safe. Sometimes she becomes safe because the perpetrator gets the right help and is no longer a perpetrator. Sometimes she becomes safe because she manages to finally leave.

On the outside, the survivor looks normal to family, friends, and supporters who want to help but don't really know how. So they advise her "get on" with her life, now that she is safe.

The simple truth is that the survivor can't just "get on" with her life.

- She needs to process her predicament and make some sense of it.
- She has a profound need to reorient to life itself.

There is much work to be done before a victim becomes a survivor—and even more work before she can thrive and triumph.

Life after abuse is never the same as it was before. When trauma happens, the victim experiencing the trauma is often busy surviving or simply moving through the stages of shock, horror, or grief.

- The world as the victim knows it is shattered and falls messily into disjointed bits and pieces.
- Things don't make sense and nothing comforts.
- When at last the survivor is safe, her life as she knew it is now over.

Abuse, especially repetitive abuse, leaves a lasting "impression" — a "bruise" that never fades — on the health, well-being, and post-abuse functioning of the victim. This impact lingers long after the actual bruises fade, the bones mend, and the abuse is over.

Still, many domestic violence survivors don't understand the lasting effects of violence. Neither do many of their friends and relatives, and neither do the people who serve them in the domestic violence advocacy, medical, and law enforcement communities. Most of these do not understand how significantly this lingering *imprint* of violence is affecting the survivor's well-being and her ability to function and carry on a normal life.

If you are a survivor, or if you are supporting a survivor who is stuck in the survivor stage, you need to realize that there is still work to do before a survivor can become a victor. That's because the aftermath of domestic violence is still extracting a high price.

---

It ain't over 'til it's over.

— *Yogi Berra*

It's not over until it's over. And even then it's not over.

— *Jesse Jackson*

---

Domestic violence is not over until justice has been served. *And even then, it's not over.* It's not over until you are safe, justice has been served, and *you are well.*

To get to the next stage, you *must become well.* As long as you continue to suffer from the numerous ills of domestic violence, your ability to function and adequately care for yourself and your children is severely compromised and impaired.

## The victor stage

Victors take the pain of their past abuse and transform it into success. When they do so, they gain a state of robust wellness and functioning.

---

What does not destroy me makes me stronger.

— *Friedrich Nietzsche*

---

In medicine it is a well-recognized fact that after broken bones mend, the bone is stronger at the site of the fracture.

Motivational speakers and writers have about a thousand different ways to assure us that:

The success that follows failure or profound disappointment is always greater than a first-time-around success that occurred without encountering any obstacles at all.

You've probably heard the old, much-given advice: "When life hands you a lemon, make lemonade." The advisor's recipe for lemonade never seems to accompany this good philosophy, however.

So, suppose you have never made lemonade and don't have a clue how to handle the lemons. You don't know how to combine them with the other necessary ingredients. Suppose also that there are no known recipes for lemonade. The good, cooling drink might never get made.

Fortunately there are ways to "make lemonade" as well as ways to win a transformation for you.

This book won't give you all the ways to make lemonade and accomplish your desired transformation. It *will* get you started by providing you with Five Ways that have worked for others in the past.

# Your transformation toolkit

Your transformation toolkit is made up of both mental and equipment resources, starting out with your positive mindset.

### Start out with a positive mindset

The survivor who says she can become a victor and the survivor who says she can't become a victor have one thing in common. They are both right. How we think is how we act.

> If you think you can do a thing or think you can't do a thing, you're right.
>
> — *Henry Ford*

## Intend to become a victor

You will be successful when you make the intention to become a victor. Intentions drive accomplishment. Add to that intention a strong healthy dose of patience and persistence and you are ready to prepare for your journey.

> Each decision we make, each action we take, is born out of an intention.
>
> — *Sharon Salzberg*

## Get a new journal or notebook

Before you start to read the rest of this book, I recommend that you give yourself the present of a new notebook or journal. Make that journal or notebook your constant companion. You can use the notebook to:

- Log your progress.
- Do the WellWriting exercises you will learn throughout this book.
- Capture insights that come to you during the day.

You can use the lines in this book as a notebook, too. When you need to write more, use your notebook to keep writing.

### *Your notebook*

 Whenever you see this book symbol anywhere in the book, a writing exercise is coming up. If you want to skip the talk and get right to the job, scan for the notebook symbol shown here.

It's a good idea to take your notebook to your bedside nightstand when you retire for the night. That way, you can easily record those dreams that whisper answers in the middle of the night.

There are many ways to success in your transformational journey. This book will show you Five Ways.

- Along your path to success, you may learn other Ways from different companions along the path.
- You might even discover new Ways that you have never heard about before.

When this happens, I'd like to hear from you. Please take the time to visit the Health After Trauma website (www.healthaftertrauma.com) to share your discoveries with me and others, or email me at DrT@healthaftertrauma.com.

## It's all up to you

Self-help books come in all shapes and sizes carrying advice, encouragement, and good wishes for you the reader. What all these books have in common is this shared wisdom:

- In the end, the only person who can help you is *you*.
- You can't change what happened to you, but you can change what you are doing with it.
- Most important, you can change what you will do in the future.

## Marshal your resources

Years ago, I found myself in a terrible dilemma, one that had the makings for big financial trouble as well as the loss of a cherished dream. Advice from J. Paul Getty saved me. I didn't know him, but I had read one of his books. As writer Natalie Goldberg said of a favorite of hers, in her audio book *Thunder and Lightning: Cracking Open the Writer's Craft,* "I met his mind."

Getty's advice for times of trouble was this: "In times of crisis, do not panic, but marshal all your resources."

Many writers have talked about the Chinese character for the word *crisis,* which seems to be the combination of two other characters: one for *danger* and one for *opportunity.* Although many successful people report that they have indeed found opportunity in the midst of crisis, at least one Chinese scholar disagrees, saying there is no *opportunity* in the Chinese character for *crisis.*

J. Paul Getty wrote that you can turn crisis into opportunity by marshalling the resources you already have and using them to confront the crisis before you.

### Start by making some lists

When you feel you have a crisis, that's the time to go on an *opportunity hunt.*

Start by making a list of all your resources that you have for undertaking the journey to becoming a victor. You can either write in spaces furnished in this book or make an entry in your journal.

## My Resources

*My natural gifts*

_____

_____

_____

_____

_____

_____

_____

_____

_____

_____

_____

_____

_____

_____

_____

_____

_____

_____

_____

_____

_____

_____

_____

_____

_____

_____

_____

*My financial resources*

_____

_____

_____

_____

_____

_____

_____

_____

_____

_____

_____

_____

_____

_____

_____

_____

_____

_____

_____

_____

_____

_____

_____

*My people resources (supporters)*

_____

_____

_____

_____

_____

_____

_____

_____

_____

_____

_____

_____

_____

_____

_____

_____

_____


*My skills*

_____

_____

_____

_____

_____

_____

_____

_____

_____

_____

_____

_____

_____

_____

_____

_____

_____

_____

_____

*Other resources*

_____

_____

_____

_____

_____

_____

_____

_____

_____

_____

_____

_____

_____

_____

---
---
---
---

## Wrapup

In this chapter you learned:

- About the toll that abuse and trauma takes on your health and functioning
- What's in a Way
- About the stages of coping with abuse and trauma
- What's in your transformation toolkit
- About the need to take charge of your journey

Now it's time to take a look at the First Way: WellWriting.

# Way One:

# WellWriting

## Nora's story

**Nora was 32 when she rediscovered** an old college friend at a book signing. Kurt was tall, charming, and intelligent. Nora and Kurt went for coffee after the book signing. During their college catch-up session, they realized how much they were enjoying the company of each other.

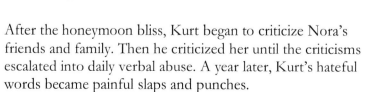

Soon the two were dating. Kurt often took flowers to Nora's office and took her on enjoyable outings. After a year of a most wonderful courtship, Nora married Kurt. Their marriage seemed idyllic to her family and friends.

After the honeymoon bliss, Kurt began to criticize Nora's friends and family. Then he criticized her until the criticisms escalated into daily verbal abuse. A year later, Kurt's hateful words became painful slaps and punches.
The day Kurt pushed Nora down the stairs and threatened to kill her dog was the day she awakened to her plight.

The next day, while Kurt was at work, she packed and left with the dog to move in with her mother in another city. She arranged for a lawyer to deal with Kurt and get a divorce.

Kurt was having an affair at his office and actually viewed Nora's departure as good riddance. As Kurt settled into his new love and life, Nora was left with long days trying to figure out what had happened to her. The trauma of her divorce piled on top of the trauma of her abuse. Nora no longer knew who she was and felt totally disoriented from life.

As a survivor of trauma and abuse, you know Nora's plight all too well. What you might not know was Nora's savior, which turned out to be a journal and pen.

Nora began to write frequently in her journal. She wrote:

- To find out how her marriage went wrong
- To understand the person she had become
- Most of all, to learn how to put her life back together and jumpstart her career

Nora later told friends and family that these excursions into her journal literally saved her life.

# Writing for your health and improvement

In this chapter you will discover:

- The healing power of writing
- The value and power of telling your story
- How to use writing to define the change you need and to log your progress
- How to use writing as therapy

## The healing power of writing

You can write yourself well—or at least better. Writing as a health tool goes by several names: journaling, expressive writing, therapeutic writing and emotive writing.

Research by psychologist James Pennebaker from the University of Texas in Austin, and by others in the healthcare field, has proven that such writing is a therapeutic tool. Their research reveals the positive effects of writing to discharge negative and harmful emotions associated with past trauma.

Improvement of various physical and mental conditions has been reported in several patient populations through the use of control studies. To date improvement has been shown for asthma, arthritis, chronic pain syndromes and chronic fatigue syndrome, just to name a few.

Does it work? In the summer 2004 issue of *Clinical Psychology: Science & Practice,* Dr. Pennebaker notes that expressive writing has in general produced good results, but the real puzzle is why does expressive writing work and how?

To date, there has not been a single theory produced to explain why it works. This, in part, may be because expressive writing affects those who engage in it on many different levels: mentally, emotionally, physically, and socially.

Still, we know some things about journaling or expressive writing. Such writing leads to self-disclosure that helps you identify your problems and recognize their emotional impact on you.

- Experiences that cause you trauma can lead you to have intricate, complex, and distressful feelings.
- To complicate matters, others who underwent the same trauma at the same time may be impacted entirely differently.

What a mystery that some are affected one way while others go free of lingering emotion.

Want to learn more about expressive writing from the researcher who validated its effectiveness? Read Dr. James Pennebaker's book, *Writing to Heal: A Guided Journal for Recovering from Trauma and Emotional Upheaval.*

## Deep inside, we know

I believe that free writing or expressive writing works because, deep inside, *we know*, but we don't know that we know. When you write quickly without editing, you produce a flow of words that unleashes your inner self and give it permission to "tell all." Your reward is the occasional "aha!," along with amazing revelations. Your writing discoveries will tell you who you are, reveal why you got that way and point to the discovery of your mission in life.

Years ago, I heard Gloria Steinem give an interview about her book on self-esteem. She said that we teach what we need to learn and we write what we need to know. How true.

— *Dr. T*

# The value and power of telling your story

What Nora did was simply to tell her story. The importance of doing this cannot be emphasized enough. As psychologist Linda Daniels writes in her book, *Healing Journeys,* you begin to heal and recover from trauma when you remember and own your entire experience. As you write, recall all the reactions your experience provoked:

- Emotional
- Physical
- Thoughts
- Spiritual effects

> There is no agony like bearing an untold story inside of you.
>
> — *Trauma survivor Maya Angelou*

# My Story

*Try writing now. Using this book or your notebook, begin to tell your own story.*

_____

_____

_____

_____

_____

_____

_____

_____

_____

_____

_____

_____

_____

_____

_____

_____

_____

_____

_____

_____

Does the writing make you feel bad? That's okay. Sometimes you just have to feel worse before you can feel better. You can write and cry, though be careful that the page you are writing on doesn't get too soggy.

## A painful vacation

An acquaintance recently told me what she learned when she wrote about her African vacation. She said, "It was on that trip that our 23-year-old marriage began to unravel.

"For the sake of the children, we managed to get through another year, but then the kids were grown and away so we went ahead and got a divorce. This confused our children, who didn't understand why we couldn't go on together.

"So I began the story of our vacation and wrote about all the things that had gone wrong. It was very painful and it made me feel bad. But then later, I felt better. I had new insights that began to explain to me why all this had happened."

In the end, she decided not to show the story she had written to her children. So my friend kept the insights and threw away the paper the story was written on.

## Writing and rewriting

Most good writers will tell you that the writing is not in the writing. The writing is in the *rewriting*.

- Write your story over and over.
- As a survivor of abuse, you have experienced trauma over and over again. Each traumatic experience has its own story just as you are your own story.
- Your story is the summation of all that has happened to you, both good and bad, and what you did with what happened to you.
- Remember that your story is always in the making. This very minute is the beginning of the rest or your story.

## It's never too late to tell your story

Henriette Anne Klauser, PhD, in her book *With Pen in Hand; the Healing Power of Writing,* tells of her friend Cassie. At the age of 42, Cassie sought counseling for emotional distress that lingered on after she had been sexually assaulted.

At the end of the first session, the therapist gave Cassie a book about what happens to crime victims. At the end of the second session, the counselor advised Cassie to write her story of the rape. That was Cassie's breakthrough.

Dr. Klauser quotes psychotherapist Kathleen Adams, author of *The Way of the Journal:*

Four therapeutic components are necessary to recover from sexual abuse:

- Explore feelings
- Mourn violation
- Gather strength
- Celebrate healing

Cassie had accomplished each of these when she committed the story of her trauma to paper.

## Where have you been and where do you need to go?

Your current story is not only about what happened to you, but how what happened has impacted you and changed your life.

*Here's what happened to me and what I did with it.*

_____

_____

_____

_____

_____

_____

_Here's where I am now in my life and in my journey of healing._

*Now I'll write the rest of my story: Where do I intend to go?*

_____

_____

_____

_____

_____

_____

_____

_____

_____

_____

_____

_____

_____

_____

_____

_____

_____

_____

_____

If, after experiencing severe trauma or sustained abuse, you are in superb health and function at your fullest potential, you can still write about an even better you.

It's your story and you have the right to tell it.

## The impact of telling your story

Write your story again and again as the days go by. Each time you write what happened to you, write a story about how what happened impacted you. Each time you write your story and tell its impact, new insights often arise. More details of the buried past are excavated and put in the spotlight.

Writing about your trauma and past hurt gets the pain out in the open. This gives you the upper hand in dealing with the chronic pain and depression that frequently follows past trauma and abuse.  Remember:

> If you bring forth that which is within you,
> Then that which is within you
> Will be your salvation.
> If you do not bring forth that which is within you,
> Then that which is within you
> Will destroy you.
>
> — *Christ*
> *Secret Gospel of Saint Thomas*

- If chronic pain or depression (or both) prevents you from living a full life, then the pain or depression has *you* and is winning. It is your enemy.

- When the enemy is seen, its power is diminished. It can be addressed, not feared. When you can see and address the enemy, its ability to sabotage you is diminished.

## *Write about the changes you can make*

 Now that you have written your story and identified how it impacted you, it is time to take action. Start by writing about the changes that might help you want to improve your health and life. Write quickly and without thinking. No idea is too far out. Just brainstorm away. Don't stop until you have at least 25 ideas written down.

*Changes I can make*

_____

_____

_____

_____

_____

_____

_____

_____

_____

_____

_____

_____

_____

_____

_____

_____

_____

_____

_____

_____

_____

_____

When you finish your list, set it aside and then come back to it later. When you see the list again, you will discover that no matter how far out some of the ideas seemed at the time, there is at least one gem there that will help you improve.

## Log your progress day by day

Putting that one gem of change to work is like taking a new journey. Many studies that focus on change note that change is more likely to be successful and continued when your progress is charted. This allows you to monitor your progress and make course corrections as you proceed.

*Captain's log*

A log is a record of a journey recorded at the end of each day. What did you see? What happened? The log records past events and tells how the captain changed the ship's course when needed.

*My day-to-day progress*

_____

_____

_____

_____

_____

_____

_____

_____

_____

_____

_____

_____

_____

_____

_____

_____

_____

_____

_____

_____

_____

_____

_____

## How to use writing to define the change you need and to log your progress

Change is not a single event but an event composed of stages. Change is not easy, but it is possible. In their book, _Changing for Good,_ psychologists Prochaska, Norcross, and DiClemente note that successful change usually doesn't happen all at once, but in stages.

First, you must gain awareness that there is a problem that needs to be overcome. At this stage, action is not the next step but rather preparation for that action. Then when the action is undertaken, it must be maintained.

 ### _Write about results_

- To maintain the action you are taking, you must constantly examine the results you are getting.
- Write constantly for maximal success.
- Write about what is harder and what is easier than you expected.
- Write kind and compassionate words of encouragement to yourself.

*Now that I am taking action, what results am I getting?*

_____

_____

_____

_____

_____

_____

_____

_____

_____

_____

_____

_____

*Now that I am taking action, what is easier than I expected?*

_____

_____

_____

_____

_____

_____

_____

_____

_____

_____

_____

_____

_____

_____

_____

*Now that I am taking action, what is harder than I expected?*

_____

_____

_____

_____

_____

_____

_____

_____

_____

_____

_____

_____

_____

_____

_____

_____

_____

_____

_____

*Write yourself a pep talk. Use as many kind and compassionate words as you can.*

_____

_____

_____

_____

_____

_____

_____

_____

_____

_____

_____

_____

_____

_____

_____

_____

_____

_____

_____

_____

In addition to charting your progress, make lists of successes and obstacles that you are encountering.

Use your log as a journal — a daily diary — as well as for telling your story. Write about your successes as well as the challenges. Tell what happened when you tried to overcome those challenges.

*My successes in life*

_____

_____

_____

_____

_____

_____

_____

_____

_____

_____

_____

_____

_____

_____

_____

_____

*Challenges I face*

_____

_____

_____

_____

_____

_____

_____

_____

_____

_____

## Try mind-storming

 If you hit a solid obstacle in your writing, try *mind-storming.* This is a technique where you write down a question and then, writing very quickly, so fast that you write and don't think, write at least 25 things to try out.

### *Write quickly*

- Don't read or judge.
- Just write.
- Write at least 25 things to try out.
- After you stop writing, take a few minutes to review the answers.

*An example of mind-storming: Write 25 (or more) activities you can try out in your life.*

_____

_____

_____

_____

_____

_____

_____

_____

_____

_____

_____

_____

_____

_____

_____

_____

_____

_____

_____

_____

_____

_____

_____

_____

Often you will find that something you have written will guide you, or will give you an "aha!" realization. On days when you strike out, be patient and set that particular question aside. Then return to the question again a few days later.

### What happens if you feel you "fall off the wagon" when you undertake change?

 When you fall off the wagon, you may feel that you are not succeeding. Actually, you are. Falling off the wagon is not a terminal event. It is just a setback.

- Write about what caused you to fall off the wagon and how you felt when you did.

- Then, get back up, forgive yourself, and get back on your writing wagon.

*What caused me to fall off the wagon and how did that make me feel?*

_____

_____

_____

_____

_____

_____

_____

_____

_____

_____

_____

_____

_____

_____

*What's the best way to get back on the wagon and not fall off again?*

_____

_____

_____

_____

_____

_____

_____

_____

_____

_____

_____

_____

_____

_____

_____

Successful change is so sprinkled with setbacks and challenges that many authors who write about change prefer to call these setbacks not *relapses* but *recycles*. Remember what the diet experts tell us when we eat that big piece of chocolate cake: "Success begins again at the next meal."

## How to use your writing as therapy

Dr. Klauser, in her book *With Pen in Hand: The Healing Power of Writing*, presents another example of writing and wellness. Dr. Klauser tells the story of Debra, a previous victim of domestic violence.

When Debra's marriage of 16 years fell apart, she and her children were "shocked, traumatized, and sad." Then Debra began to write and write in her journal.

One of her first entries spoke to her physical condition:

> "My body manifested my pain. …. My skin erupted in a miserable rash and my eyes were swollen shut. Strange how emotional suffering can become so physical."

Another puzzling thing that happened to Debra after her husband left was that she began to have severe migraine headaches. She couldn't imagine why the headaches were occurring then but not when she was still being abused. However, as Dr. Klauser notes, it "is not an unusual symptom for those who have gotten out of a dangerous situation, but have not dealt with the aftermath."

Debra did use her writing to ultimately resolve and accept her situation, deal with the confusion and ambiguity of her emotions, and develop the wisdom not to return to her abuser when he returned and asked her to come back. Debra's advice on why to write is summed up with:

"Writing is something you can do for yourself. It's not expensive, and it doesn't hurt anybody, but you can gain personal benefit from it." She ends by laughing and offers this advice, "You can't afford a therapist? Write."

# Wrapup

In this chapter you learned about:

- The healing power of writing
- The value and power of telling your story

- How to use writing to define the change you need and to log your progress
- How to experience writing as therapy

# Way Two:

# Manage Your Anger

Anybody can become angry — that is easy;
but to be angry with the right person,
and to the right degree,
and at the right time,
and for the right purpose,
and in the right way—
that is not within everybody's power
and is not easy.

— Aristotle

# Let's look at anger

Do you sometimes feel that you no longer have anger, but anger has you? In this chapter you will learn ways to handle your anger by learning to:

- Harness and use your anger
- Listen and learn from your anger
- Forgive those who have hurt you
- Release your anger
- Discover your hidden emotions

## Harness and use your anger

Here is a secret: Anger can be good, and anger can be bad.

One secret to becoming a victor, not a victim, lies in being aware of what is good and just anger and what is bad and destructive anger.

- Mastery comes from learning how to use the good anger and how to diminish and release the bad anger.
- You need to learn when to *use* anger and when to *lose* it.

## Fear is one of the roots of anger

Anger is a natural reaction to threatening, provoking or belittling circumstances. The common root of anger is *fear*. Fear can be very personal. What scares some, barely fazes others.

---

## We boil at different degrees.

*— Ralph Waldo Emerson*

---

What matters is what angers *you* and what you can do about it.

Survivors are no strangers to anger. Anger is often associated with three common conditions plaguing survivors:

- Chronic pain
- Post-Traumatic Stress Disorder (PTSD)
- Depression

If you have any of these three conditions, you will need to learn to handle your anger. Then you can expect improvement in the severity of your medical condition.

You will have more resources to cope and heal when anger does not cloud your vision and occupy your life.

# The good and bad of anger

There are two sides to anger: good and bad.

## The good

> To be angry is very good. It burns out things and leaves nutrients in the soil.
>
> You should always be ready to be angry at injustice and cruelty.
>
> — *Maya Angelou*

- In 1979, a mother was left with an infant quadriplegic daughter when their car was hit by a repeat drunk driver offender traveling at 120 miles an hour.

- Almost a year later, a mother in Sacramento, California, lost her 13 year-old daughter to a drunk driver who was a known repeat offender.

These mothers, a "loosely assembled group of brokenhearted mothers," and some of their friends formed a new organization: Mothers Against Drunk Driving (MADD).

According to their website, MADD has gone from being a small group of women to a nationwide organization with over 600 chapters. Since its start in 1980, more than 2,300 anti-drunk driving laws have been passed.

In a 1994 study made by the Chronicle of Philanthropy, MADD was the most popular non-profit cause in the U.S., well liked by 51 percent of Americans. It ranked second among the most strongly supported charities and third on the most credible list.

What a difference anger can make when harnessed and channeled. It becomes the rocket fuel of healthy change.

### *Have you ever used anger to heal?*

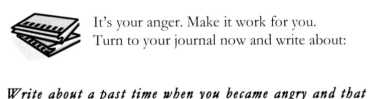 It's your anger. Make it work for you.
Turn to your journal now and write about:

*Write about a past time when you became angry and that anger inspired change that caused you to be healthier.*

_____

_____

_____

_____

_____

_____

_____

_____

_____

_____

_____

_____

_____

_____

_____

_____

_____

_____

_____

_____

_____

*Write about what anger you have now and explore how you might harness and channel that anger.*

_____

_____

_____

_____

_____

_____

_____

_____

_____

_____

_____

_____

_____

_____

_____

_____

_____

_____

_____

_____

President Harry Truman had an interesting way to vent his anger. When his anger flared, he would immediately fire off a letter that would vent his anger. Then, instead of sending the letter, he would store the letters together in their own "unsent file." Anger spent, he then cooled down and wrote the letter that he actually sent. (Wouldn't you just love to see the ones he didn't send?)

> # Caution!
>
> Write it…
>
> But don't send it.

*Try these exercises*

*Write a letter to a person or an institution that made you angry.*

_____

_____

_____

_____

_____

_____

_____

_____

_____

_____

_____

_____

_____

_____

_____

_____

_____

_____

_____

_____

_____

_____

_____

_____

_____

_____

_____

*Write a "letter to the editor" of your local newspaper about your anger and what you think should be done about it.*

_____

_____

_____

_____

_____

_____

_____

_____

_____

_____

_____

_____

*See your anger as a "lemon" life has handed you, and then write up several recipes for lemonade that you will make with this lemon.*

_____

_____

_____

_____

_____

_____

_____

_____

_____

_____

_____

_____

_____

_____

_____

_____

_____

_____

_____

_____

_____

_____

_____

_____

_____

_____

_____

_____

_____

*List all the "wrongs" of the act or situation that caused you to be angry.*

_____

_____

_____

_____

_____

_____

_____

_____

_____

_____

_____

_____

_____

_____

_____

_____

## The bad

> Anger and hatred are the materials from
> which hell is made.
>
> — *Thich Nhat Hanh*

> Holding on to anger is like grasping a hot coal
> with the intent of throwing it at someone else —
> You are the one who gets burned.
>
> — *The Buddha*

> Anger blows out the lamp of the mind.
>
> — *Robert G. Ingersoll*

> Anger and intolerance are the enemies of correct understanding.
>
> — *Mahatma Gandhi*

Although anger can be a positive and good emotion if handled appropriately, there are long-time physical costs of uncontrolled anger produced from the constant flood of stress chemicals coursing through your body.

Anger, anxiety, fear, and grief are all forms of chronic stress. This chronic stress can keep your nervous system perpetually aroused. This constant and prolonged stress has been shown to contribute to illness and immune changes in both humans and animals.

The health problems that can result from unmanaged anger include:

- Headache
- Digestion problems, such as abdominal pain
- Insomnia
- Increased anxiety
- Depression
- High blood pressure
- Skin problems, such as eczema
- Heart attack
- Stroke

So in the end, getting your anger under control and ridding yourself of the anger wherever possible will result in a healthier you — a victor.

Fortunately, the library is full of books
that can help you deal with anger.

Some techniques for dealing with anger
and healing from its harmful effects
include:

- Learning from the anger
- Forgiving (not forgetting)
- Releasing the anger

## Listen and learn from your anger

> It is wise to focus your anger on problems, not people.
> Focus your energies on answers, not excuses.
>
> — *William Arthur Ward*

Anger has power. It organizes your environment, often in
harmful ways in the world of cause and effect.

At the same time anger clouds your own mind and vision.
Don't fail to overlook its one major asset: What angers you has
meaning.

Seminar leader John-Richard Turner taught me a valuable
lesson in 1984: "Whenever you find yourself angry, ask
yourself this question: 'What does this say about me that I am
afraid might be true?'"

When John-Richard first said this, it made no sense whatsoever
to me. Some clarification came when he was challenged by a

young mother who told him that she got angry when her three-year-old-son would wander away and not return when she called him back.

John-Richard explained that it was the nature of mothers to protect their children, while at the same time young boys eventually went to explore the world and be absorbed in it. "Your anger," John-Richard told the mother, "comes from your fear that you are losing your power over your young son and thus your ability to protect him."

I filed away and forgot this bit of advice for a year or so. Then I moved to another city and became a Chairman of Emergency Medicine in a busy teaching hospital. The residency program — a training program for physicians — was in danger of disappearing and had been put on probation for the third and last time. We had much work to do to save the program.

Change is hard, especially when it involves more night shifts, requisite research projects, and the loss of moon-lighting time. Our residents were not happy and kept sending provoking letters with demands to me and the faculty.

The demands couldn't be met, but they could sure make me angry. Then one day I got a new set of demands, and before I knew it I was over the top with anger.

There was nothing to do for it but take a hike and hope that walking would burn off the anger. While strolling about, I suddenly heard John-Richard's voice. Ask the question his voice urged. So I did. I stopped and said to myself, "So what do these demands say to me that I am afraid might be true?"

My inner voice responded so fast that I suspected it had been lurking in the shadows, waiting for a chance to pipe up. "What you are afraid of," said that little inner whisper, "is that you don't know what you are doing."

There it was — a fear out in the open. Relief flooded in: Why *should* I know what I was doing? I had never been a chairman before. It was no secret that I was new to the job and on a learning curve. My anger melted and with it came the balm of relief.

The clarity of the moment of fading anger gave me some time to figure out how to best deal with future demands. I devised a plan: The next time a letter of demand was handed to me, I simply handed it back, unopened, and said to the residents, "I don't do demands. But I do listen to concerns and like suggestions. My open door policy extends to you as well as the faculty."

The upshot was very rewarding. The residents stopped sending the letters and many did come see me with their concerns and suggestions. By the time they graduated and left our program, each one of them held a special place in my heart.

 ### *Write about anger*

In your journal, write about your anger. When you do this:

- Remember to just write and write. Let the words stomp about and then soar off the page.
- Write out your fears.
- Write out your anger.
- Write everything out — and keep writing…

*Write about something that makes you very angry. Then write the answer to this question: "What does this say about me that I am afraid might be true?"*

_____

_____

_____

_____

_____

_____

_____

_____

_____

_____

_____

_____

_____

_____

_____

_____

_____

_____

_____

_____

_____

_____

_____

_____

_____

_____

_____

_____

_____

_____

> Let us not look back in anger or forward in fear, but around in awareness.
>
> — *James Thurber*

## Let your anger inform you

Make a regular habit of letting your anger inform you. When you do this, you will become more aware of what is happening and more aware of life and your own sense of meaning. Awareness lets you live in the healthy state of the here and now.

The ancient wisdom of awareness is reflected in Buddhist practice. "Buddha" means "enlightened one," one who perceives within his or her own being the essence, or reality of life.

When Shakyamuni Buddha was still alive, people came to him and asked, "What are you? A God, a saint, an angel?" His response was simple, "I am awake."

On one occasion the Buddha was asked if he could sum up his teachings in only a few words. It only took one: *awareness*. Be aware. Be here. Be now.

# Forgive those who have hurt you

This is a tough one. Remember that forgiveness for others as well as for yourself promotes well being, peace of mind, and your health. Not forgiving results in grudge-holding that builds up anger, depression, and anxiety.

Be aware that forgiveness does not mean forgetting or playing that the wrong done to you never happened. It did happen. It may not be your fault that you were wronged, but it is your responsibility to accept and deal with what happened.

Reading about forgiveness is far easier than actually forgiving. This is because forgiving is not an innate skill or state of being. Fortunately, the art of forgiveness can be learned, as researchers at the *Stanford Forgiveness Project* have demonstrated.

Dr. Fred Luskin, who heads the Stanford Project, recommends four steps for you to acquire forgiveness. These four steps, paraphrased, are summarized here:

- Experience the anger and then realize you have a choice how to respond to the situation.
- Realize the anger you have does not feel good and is hurting your health.
- Release the anger as quickly as you can.
- Vow to proactively forgive in the future.

# Release your anger

> Holding on to anger only gives you tense muscles.
>
> *— Joan Lunden*

The first two steps recommended by Dr. Luskin are simple compared to the last two. Success in these areas involves accepting life as it is: a series of repetitions.

The braggart in your workplace will continue to brag, the bully will continue to bully, and the complainer will continue to complain. If there is preventive action to take, take it. Tell the bully to back off in the future, ask the bragger to brag elsewhere, and ask the complainer to complain in private.

These actions may or may not work, but you know that you have done something to change the situation. Then you need to embrace the awareness that you have choice in how you will react.

Remember that these actions belong to them and not you. Or as a wise co-worker told me, "It's always about them. It's never about you."

Dr. Luskin writes that we are in the process of achieving success in the fourth stage when we find ourselves thinking thoughts such as:

- "I don't want to waste my precious life in the discomfort caused by anger, so I will choose to feel differently. I am able to forgive myself, forgive others, forgive life, and forgive God."

- "I know how it hurts when people don't forgive me. I do not want to hurt other people by my anger, so I will let it go."

- "Life is filled with incredible beauty and I am missing some if I am experiencing unresolved anger. I forgive myself for getting sidetracked."

- "People do the best they can and if they err I can best help them by offering understanding. The first step in this process is to forgive the specific offense."

## Can't release your anger?

> Never answer a letter while you are angry.
>
> — *Chinese Proverb*

I mentioned former U.S. President Harry Truman earlier. He must have known of this Chinese proverb because he had a rule: Any letter he wrote when angry had to sit on his desk for

24 hours before it could be mailed. This "moratorium" allowed him to review these letters after he had cooled off.

If the letter read okay to him when he was calm, he would mail the letter. If not, President Truman would simply drop the letter into a drawer. At the time of his death, his unmailed letters filled up a large drawer. Eventually, they were published in a book, *Strictly Personal and Confidential: The Letters Harry Truman Never Mailed.*

## Hidden emotions

Suppose you have a boss who makes you very angry. Yet you cannot afford to directly express your anger and have yet to find another way to express it or let it go.

Your friends and co-workers might think all is well, but you know down deep that you have the anger and for now choose to live with it or deal with it in another manner. Your anger at your boss is a known emotion.

But did you know that you can have hidden emotions that you don't feel or even know that you have? Samuel J. Mann, MD, in his book *Healing Hypertension: A Revolutionary New Approach,* asserts that some patients with hypertension resolve their condition when hidden emotions are flushed out and dealt with.

Dr. Mann has treated many hypertensive patients at the Hypertension Center of the New York Presbyterian Hospital/Cornell Medical Center. His patients were referred to him because conventional therapy had failed. It is important to note that Dr. Mann doesn't write that *all* hypertension is caused by hidden emotions. However, he does maintain that in some patients, hypertension does resolve when they explore, find, and deal with their hidden emotions.

Of interest, Dr. Mann notes that he sees many patients who deny being tense, angry, or depressed on their psychological questionnaires, and yet they have these same feelings showing on their faces. These are the at-risk folks for high blood pressure who do not respond to conventional treatment.

### *Write about what makes you mad*

Might you have hidden anger that you don't know about?

*In your journal, make a list of things that happened to you that would normally make you or others angry.*

_____

_____

_____

_____

_____

_____

_____

_____

_____

_____

_____

_____

_____

_____

_____

_____

_____

_____

_____

_____

Go back and look at your list.

- Beside each event, write an anger score.
- A score of 0 represents no anger felt at all.
- A score of one is barely perceptible anger, the last dying ashes in a campfire going completely out.
- A score of 10 would represent a raging forest fire.

### *Followup*

Take the one event that you scored highest and then write for 15 minutes about how you feel.

Let your feelings out. Connect with your feelings and then you can experience them, learn from them, and let them go.

*Start with, "After all this time, I still feel......"*

_____

_____

_____

_____

_____

_____

_____

_____

_____

_____

_____

_____

_____

_____

_____

_____

_____

_____

_____

_____

_____

## Wrapup

In this chapter, you have now explored ways to master your anger. Use your journal to free-write ways to:

- Harness and use your anger
- Listen and learn from your anger
- Forgive those who have hurt you
- Release your anger
- Discover your hidden emotions

# Way Three:

# Live Well With Stress

## Meg's Story

**When Meg left her abusive partner,** John, she discovered that leaving was not a simple process, but it was possible. John had never hit her, but his verbal violence and unexpected outbursts of anger had Meg feeling as if she were walking on eggshells all the time. So after a while Meg left.

John called and made promises to change. When Meg refused to return, John's promises gave way first to pleading and then to anger, and then to the familiar verbal taunts she was trying to escape.

After two weeks of phone calls, John called and screamed into the phone, "You can have your stupid divorce. I never want to see you or hear from you again. You will always be sorry for doing this. Your selfishness will haunt you forever."

This time, John slammed the phone down and did not call again within the hour. Meg's new phone was quiet.

The mystery of John's sudden silence became apparent the next day, when Meg learned that John had been having an affair with someone in his office, and his new friend had just become pregnant. Relief flooded over Meg because she now knew John would not bother her again.

The relief was short lived. Meg now had mounting stress coping with all the changes in her life. She had to open new banking accounts, get control of her credit cards, submit change-of-address forms, and tend to a thousand other new details, while at the same time trying to get by on only one source of income.

Yesterday's "eggshell" stress gave way to new stress. Meg began to feel she had only traded one stress for another. She began to have headaches and not sleep well. This caused her to have trouble concentrating at work. Her work production suffered and this brought on the wrath of her demanding boss.

Life had become hell. Why was she worse off, when she should be better off, now that she was free of John's constant verbal abuse?

# The challenge of stress

Did you know that stress can kill? In this chapter you will discover:

- How stress can make you sick
- How stress can force your body to say no
- How you can make the choice to master the stress in your life
- How to apply a couple of stress busters
- How to acquire some stress lifelines

# How stress can make you sick

No one lives a stress-free life. *Stress.* The word runs through all our contemporary life and language. But what does it mean to "have stress?"

Stress is the body's gift to mobilize you when you are threatened. If you perceive danger, numerous chemicals begin to flood through your body to prepare you for a fight or flight response.

That's the good news — especially if you lived in the land of saber-tooth tigers. In a split second you could respond when threatened.

Today, the saber-tooth tigers are extinct, but your body's wisdom to keep the flight or fight response persists. When real danger is at hand you are ready to go. Unfortunately, modern life provokes this reaction at times when it is neither safe nor wise to flee or fight.

The stress hormones course through your bloodstream and are not immediately used up in a flight or fight response. The results?

- Increased muscle tension
- Elevated blood pressure
- Anxiety, depression, or irritability
- A lowering of your ability to fight illness because your immune system becomes compromised

If you are a survivor of domestic violence and still caught up in the health aftermath of the abuse, there is a good chance that unbeknownst to you there is a "stress civil war" raging through your body right now.

Two very common conditions that plague many survivors are pain and stress. Both are often accompanied by depression, a condition we now know is linked with many physical expressions, including heart disease and osteoporosis. In addition, depression and chronic pain are often associated with each other and add to the level of stress that you may be experiencing.

Many survivors of trauma and abusive situations experience extreme stress in the form of post-traumatic stress disorder (PTSD) or some other variation of severe stress.

You can see how many of the key symptoms of PTSD you experience by responding to the checklist that follows. The list is based on the symptoms of PTSD identified in the PTSD expert consensus guidelines, published in the *Journal of Clinical Psychiatry* in 1999:

| Checklist: The Key Symptoms of PTSD | | |
|---|---|---|
| Symptoms | ✓ | Examples |
| Re-experiencing the traumatic event | ☐ | Intrusive, distressing recollections of the event |
| | ☐ | Flashbacks (feeling as if the event were recurring while awake) |
| | ☐ | Nightmares (the event or other frightening images recur frequently in dreams) |
| | ☐ | Exaggerated emotional and physical reactions to triggers that remind you of the event |
| Avoidance | ☐ | Of activities, places, thoughts, feelings, or conversations related to the trauma |
| Emotional numbing | ☐ | Loss of interest |
| | ☐ | Feeling detached from others |
| | ☐ | Restricted emotions |
| Increased arousal | ☐ | Difficulty sleeping |
| | ☐ | Irritability or outbursts of anger |
| | ☐ | Difficulty concentrating |
| | ☐ | Hyper-vigilance |
| | ☐ | Exaggerated startle response |

# How stress can force your body to say no

Even if you are not a survivor of abuse or trauma, you are still exposed to much stress. And there is a price to pay for unrelieved stress.

Canadian physician Gabor Matê writes of the cost of hidden stress in his fine book, *When the Body Says No.*

At the beginning of the book, the author tells of a woman who sustained severe abuse as a child. Abused children deal with a unique stress because the abuse comes from the very adults who are also their protectors and providers.

Their stress and fear teaches them to withhold self-expression and to avoid making themselves vulnerable. Their very security depends on constantly monitoring and considering the feelings and emotions of others.

This monitoring often happens at the expense of their awareness of their own needs and desires. They become completely "other" driven. The word *no* is missing from their vocabulary.

Living a life of complete concern for others while avoiding your own needs sometimes forces the body to "say no" for you. You have promised to go to a meeting or work on a project to please someone else, but when the time comes for you to deliver, a raging headache takes over your whole life and brings you down.

The headache may be painful, but it can also be serving a purpose. If the body is not given the chance to recover, it reacts. It may find temporary relief when your severe pain takes over and you are forced to rest and recover the toll of built up stress.

When relief and recovery are not possible, the body struggles for balance and survival. The resulting struggle can set in motion a slow downward spiral.

It's time for you to learn how your body says "no" to you. You want to learn:

- What physical ailments are costing you?
- Which ailments are worse?
- Why is your body using these particular ailments?
- What successful coping techniques are available to address your ailments?

 Go to your notebook now to seek answers to these questions.

*List what physical ailments you had recently that caused you to miss going to work or working on a project that you wanted to finish.*

_____

_____

_____

_____

_____

_____

_____

_____

_____

_____

_____

_____

_____

*Did each ailment occur only once or more than once? Was one more severe than the others? If so, which one?*

_____

_____

_____

_____

_____

_____

_____

_____

_____

_____

_____

_____

_____

*Pick the ailment that appeared the most or hurt the most and write about that. How did it feel? Why did your body choose this ailment rather than another to bring you to a state of rest and recovery?*

_____

_____

_____

_____

_____

_____

_____

_____

_____

_____

_____

_____

_____

_____

_____

_____

*Do you know of anyone else who suffers with the same ailments? If so, what coping technique does she use to deal with this same ailment? If not, where might you turn to find coping techniques for these ailments?*

## Write your story now weaving in the ailments that you identified

Now that you have warmed up your writing engine answering these questions, it is time to be an author and write your story. Start anywhere. Your story might start like this:

> The beast in my head appeared, like a thunderclap of pain and heat while I was brushing my teeth to get ready for work. The white hot poker in my head took over everything. I next remember lying on the couch. Roger, my boss, appeared in my mind and was yelling at me: "Where is your report? Don't you know this is the big day. What kind of _____" His voice became walled away behind the pain. I no longer heard him. I only heard the throbbing pain. The beast in my head had taken over….

OR

> I lie in bed, balanced on the heating pad down where the pain monster has grabbed my lower back. The monster was there when I got out of bed this morning. I was going to tough it out and make that meeting at work anyway. Some aspirin, maybe something stronger and I could make it. It was not to be. As soon as I stood up, pain shot down my leg. Getting to work would be impossible. Now what…

OR

> I woke up full of hope today. The big meeting that I have worked so hard for is scheduled for 9:00 a.m. My presentation is on top of my desk. I was dressed and headed to the door when pain shot through my belly. It doubled me over. What to do? I can't go on. Why now

is this pain coming? In the past it has always lasted for at least two days. I'll call Tom and he can take me to the emergency department…

 *Now write your story.*

_____

_____

_____

_____

_____

_____

_____

_____

_____

_____

_____

_____

_____

_____

_____

_____

_____

_____

## Examine your story

Once you get the beginning of your stress story out, you have
established the conflict needed for a top-notch story. You have
a goal to get to work when conflict appears in the form of an
intense, paralyzing pain. Your body has said, "no."

You are the protagonist — the heroine — of your story. Write
the story you want to *be*. To do so, the conflict has to be
resolved. A good story after all is not about the conflict, but
what the protagonist does to resolve the conflict.

- Do you win?
- Do you lose?
- Do you compromise and just continue on with life as it
  is?
- What do you do to resolve the conflict?

*My story as a winner*

_____

_____

_My story as a loser_

_____

_____

_____

_____

_____

_____

_____

*My story as a compromiser*

_____

_____

_____

_____

_____

_____

_____

_____

_____

_____

_____

_____

_____

_____

_____

*My story telling how I resolved the conflict and triumphed*

_____

_____

_____

_____

_____

_____

_____

_____

_____

_____

_____

_____

_____

_____

_____

_____

_____

_____

# How you can make the choice to master the stress in your life

All stress mastery is based on your ability to master your response to what stresses you. That is what you have most control over.

Hans Selye, author of *The Stress of Life,* is viewed by many as the father of stress research. He defines a *stressor* as an event or thing that provokes the body's fight or flight response. Stress is the result of the stressor and the person's reaction to the stress. Dr. Selye's equation of stress looks like this:

$$\text{Stress} = \text{Stressor} + \text{your response to the stressor}$$

Sometimes, when stressed, you can simply remove or modify the stressor. In one of the examples provided earlier, the stressor is a boss, Roger, who shouts at you and puts you down. Choosing to handle this stress by modifying or eliminating Roger will have limited success. You can modify Roger by telling him that you do not appreciate being yelled at and you want him to behave in the future.

While this might result in some improvement, the chances are the improvement will be minor or temporary. After all, Roger has spent his whole life handling his stress by shouting and putting others down. In addition, Roger might not take kindly to an employee who tells him how to behave. Thus this approach carries some risk.

You can quit and go in search of a new boss. This will work for a while, but the fact is that if you have a problem with people yelling at you and putting you down, it won't be long before another Roger pops up in your life.

When speaking about problems that are avoided and not dealt with, I always remember this saying:

> **If you resist (dealing with the problem),
> the problem will persist.**
>
> *— John-Richard Turner*

What you are left with here is this: the person you have the most control over is yourself. Fortunately, there are well-known stress busters and stress lifelines available to you to take control of your response to stressors in your life.

## How to apply a couple of stress busters

Learn to listen to your body. It is sending messages to you all the time. You can begin to release your stress and pain by working to answer questions like these:

- What is your body saying now? Its most powerful messages are frequently sent in the form of pain or distress. So, how do you feel?
- Do you have tension in your neck, burning in your stomach, or tightness in your back?

Once you identify this buildup of tension, you can do several things:

- Silently thank your body for sending you a signal that not all is well.
- Express appreciation for you body's innate wisdom.

- Assure your body that you have the message and will now address it.
- Tell your body that it is now safe for the pain or stress to disperse and diminish.

Once this is done, you need to get into a state of deep relaxation, as deep as you can achieve. Here's how:

- Close your eyes and take slow deep breaths. As you release each breath, feel yourself more relaxed.

- Once you feel relaxed and centered, focus your attention on the area of pain and distress. Visualize an aura of color surrounding your pain. Perhaps the color is red, the color of halt and warning.

- As you see the color, add white color to it so that it becomes less red and moves toward the color pink.

- Once you see the color pink, visualize the color changing to a color of health and healing. Common colors to represent this state are purple, violet or blue. You can even use the color green.

- Now when you let a deep breath out, see the color of the pain breaking into chunks. As you breathe out, some of the chunks leave with each breath and move into the atmosphere. Their job is done.

- The remaining chunks become lighter as their mates leave. At the very end of the process, each chunk is very light in color and freely floats away with the outgoing breath. As the chunks leave, the sensation left behind is relief and comfort.

At the end of this exercise, the pain or distress should be improved and may even be gone for now. If it's better but not gone, you can repeat this exercise as often as you wish.

Meanwhile, your job is not over. Remember the promise you made your body? You assured your body that you knew it was sending you a message and that you would "address it." If time permits, do it now. If not, do it the first time you can.

 ### *Address the pain and distress now*

Take out your journal and try this exercise:

- Title your entry with the pain or distress that you just experienced.
- Then start free-writing as fast as you can. Let the pain tell its story. Or imagine that a magical sage or wisdom child has suddenly appeared before you and is telling you the answer to that question. What is the figure saying? Be a scribe and write it all down. Here you go:
- Write for 15 to 20 minutes. No more for now. You can always return later and write more. For now, you don't want to trade your earlier pain or distress for the spasm of writer's cramp.

*What is my body trying to tell me is wrong by sending me this message?*

_____

_____

_____

_____

_____

_____

Another approach is to write answers to questions such as:

- When did I first have this type of pain?
- Have I ever been hit or hurt in this area of my body before?
- What happened to me as a child that might now be speaking to me through this pain?
- Does someone I know have pain like this? How did he or she get such a pain?
- What common language phrases incorporate this type of pain? Examples include:

> John's a pain in the ass.
> Juanita gives me a crick in my neck.
> Susan's anger makes me want to hold onto my very breath so I won't explode.
> Every time I see Stan, my stomach knots up.

## Learn to anchor yourself

This is a nice technique that you can use to quickly center yourself and break up building tension.

- Begin by getting into the deepest state of relaxation that you can achieve. Some people use self-hypnosis to do this; others just use simple relaxation techniques.
- Once you are sitting comfortably and as deeply relaxed as you can be, tell yourself that the next time you see or touch a certain object, this feeling of relaxation, warmth, and being centered will be immediately recalled by your body.
- If you choose to use a "worry stone" or other small object that fits in your pocket, you can do this exercise holding the object and actually touching it when you give yourself this command.

I think this exercise works well because the body has tremendous somatic, or "body," recall. And that recall can be used to your benefit.

Let's say you are at a carnival and you are trying to throw a ball into a bucket. You throw several times, but the ball misses the bucket or hits the rim and bounces off. Then, on one occasion *the ball lands perfectly in the bucket.* Stop right there.

- What did that feel like in your hand, arm, shoulder, stance of your body, and so on? Don't analyze the feeling. Recall it and feel it.
- Then recreate that same feeling throughout the next time you throw a ball at the bucket.

You will be surprised at how well this works.

## In the midst of excitement…

Sometimes you can anchor yourself in the midst of excitement.

When I was a faculty emergency physician at San Francisco General Hospital, I had a young resident physician who was bright and good. But when he ran his first resuscitation (a "code"), he was all over the place, giving instructions and then getting in front of the interns and disrupting them.

Later I spoke to the resident about learning to run the code by instructing the interns and not getting in their way. "Doing" was what he was supposed to do last year when he was the intern. Now he was a resident and he should be instructing.

The next resuscitation the resident ran was perfect. And the next and the next. Not only did he improve, he went from hopeless to perfect.

When I gave him this feedback he told me his secret. He went home after I spoke to him and realized that he had trouble moving from doing to instructing. So he imagined himself glued to handles of the EKG machine's table. The minute he said this, I suddenly recalled seeing him running the code, standing at the EKG machine holding onto both sides of the table, even though his feet had been dancing from side to side. What this resident did was to use the trick of holding onto the EKG machine so he wouldn't move over to the patient's bedside and disrupt what the interns were doing. Then, after the code went well, he put the EKG table into his routine. Now every time he grabbed the sides of the EKG table, he felt centered and in control. He was anchored.

## Take a break: stomp away

One good way of blowing off your stream when stressed or distressed is physical activity. Stress is the adaptation to change or threat and charges up your body for fight or flight. When that happens, you have a lot of adrenalin and other stress chemicals chugging around in your bloodstream, wiring every nerve and muscle up for intense activity.

You can just sit and let these chemicals slowly reside to normal levels, or you can get into some form of physical activity to use them up quickly.

Meg decided to run a mini-marathon and joined some friends to train together. Every morning they jogged before work.

One Friday, Meg had an early meeting and missed the training session. She promised herself that she would run as soon as she got home to make up for the missed training session. Her workday ended with a very stressful meeting.

The distress caused by the meeting was still churning away in Meg's mind and body when she got home. She got into her jogging clothes and put on her running shoes on auto-pilot and struck out for her jog.

Soon the stress of the meeting began to fade and Meg began to feel much better. She couldn't make the meeting go away by running, but her reaction to it diminished when she ran and replaced her pent-up stress chemicals with the endorphins generated by running.

*Endorphin* is the internal "narcotic" that your body produces when you run or do other steady physical activity. When runners produce internal endorphin and feel its good effects, they call the feeling a "runner's high." Dancers experience the same thing and refer to it as "dancer's bliss."

Meg soon began to schedule her stressful meetings right before lunch or as the last event of the day. Then she would put on her running clothes and run, discharging her stress chemicals and letting her worries trail behind her until they seemed small indeed.

# How to acquire some stress lifelines

Once the immediate grip of stress has been broken, it's time to build or create some stress lifelines. These are devices you use to alter your response to provocation and stress.

## Reframing stress

In work and in life, you often find yourself in situations that you find very stressful. Often these situations occur frequently over time. How do you handle that ongoing stress?

## Assess and reframe

In the first chapter, you read how a crisis may contain both danger and opportunity. When you find yourself in a situation that is stressful, concentrate on the fact that the stress is created by your *response* to the situation and not the situation itself.

## Write about the situation

So take a look at the situation that causes you stress and examine it in a new way.

- Take out your journal and enter a heading that is the name for your ongoing stress.

  In Meg's case, she would write a heading that said, "Weekly meetings with difficult-to-please boss."

- Then write a subheading called "danger." Under that, write a list of all the reasons the situation causes you to be concerned by its danger.

### Meg's list of perceived dangers

- I'll get really angry and "lose it."
- I'll get fired.
- I'll get paralyzed and unable to stand up for myself.
- I'll take it and eat it so I can keep my job, and then I'll get an ulcer.

After you make your danger list, it is time to prospect for opportunity. What good might come from this ongoing stressful situation?

### Meg's list of possible opportunities

- I can learn to take detailed notes during the meeting. It'll keep me occupied and out of trouble and I'll have my own record of what happened during the meeting and not just the official "party line."

- I can buy a book on learning to deal with difficult people and practice one technique a week. Better people skills will be mine.
- I can identify a "meeting buddy." Then we'll plan on having coffee after each meeting to vent and learn. I'll increase my social capital this way.
- I can promise myself a treat of some kind that I get every time I live through one of these meetings: a new book to read, a new CD to listen to, or a new DVD to watch at home.

As you can see, when Meg started reframing her stressful staff meetings into possible opportunities, her pen began to spill out detailed possibilities.

 **Now it's time to write**

*What is my most stressful ongoing experience?*

_____

_____

_____

_____

_____

_____

*What danger lurks in this ongoing stressful experience?*

_____

_____

_____

_____

_____

_____

*What opportunity can I find in this ongoing stressful experience?*

_____

_____

_____

_____

_____

_____

_____

_____

_____

_____

_____

_____

_____

## Reframing

Many people use reframing as an ongoing mental lifeline. Motivational speakers and authors are masters at this. Some examples:

| Situation | Situation reframed |
|---|---|
| Mistake | Learning opportunity |
| The glass is half empty | The glass is half full |
| When John leaves for college, I'll be an empty nester | Everything in the refrigerator will be all mine. |
| This car is an old clunker. | It's a great car to drive in the city. Who cares if it gets banged into? |

Notice that all these examples change the way you *perceive* a situation. The situation is still the situation.

Thomas Edison was a master at reframing. Someone once asked him how he could keep experimenting to make a light bulb when he had failed so many times. His reply:

> "Think how far ahead I am. Now I know 10,000 ways that don't work."

Reframing is the difference between being a pessimist and being an optimist. We know now that optimists live longer and are often healthier. Wouldn't you rather be an optimist?

# A Christmas Story

The depression took all the money, leaving the Schmidts' cupboards often bare. When Christmas came that year, they had money only to buy one of their twin sons a present. They decided to give the present to their son, the pessimist, because he was always so gloomy. For the other son, the optimist, there would be only an empty sock.

On Christmas Eve night, the Schmidts hung two socks on the mantle. Into the pessimist's sock went a shiny new watch. At the last minute, they couldn't bear to leave the optimist's sock empty, so the Mr. Schmidt went out to the barn to see what he could find.

He came to the empty stall for a horse had long since been sold. A few hairs from the horse's tail still dangled from a lonely nail. The father took one of the hairs and put it in the optimist's Christmas sock.

The next day dawned bright and still. The boys ran down the stairs, straight to the mantle where their socks hung.

The pessimistic twin got there first and grabbed his sock. When he saw the watch, he said, "Santa brought me a watch!" Then he dropped it and abandoned it and walked away muttering, "Probably won't work long."

The second twin then looked in his sock and slowly pulled out the lone horsehair. The parents held their breath and tried not to show their sorrow.

Suddenly a big smile appeared on the twin's face.

"Look," he cried out. "Santa brought me a pony. But he ran away." Ecstatic, he pulled on his boots, put on his coat, and skipped outside to ride his imaginary pony up and down the driveway.

## Need more stress lifelines?

Try these time-honored stress relievers:

- Listen to music.
- Read inspirational literature.
- Get a new hobby, such as knitting or needle pointing.
- Go back to school.
- Take a weekend retreat.
- See a good play or movie.
- Talk to family and friends.
- Clean house (okay, this only works for some folks)…

Whatever works for you as a stress lifeline is good.

### *In your journal, examine your stress lifelines*

- Make a list of the stress lifelines you have used in the past.
- Which ones are unhealthy, such as overeating or drinking too much?
- Take each of the unhealthy tension relievers you have used in the past and then write in your journal how you felt after you engaged in each one.
- Did they work for long, or just a bit? If they did work, did you immediately have a rebound effect?

- What price did you pay for using these stress lifelines? Did you gain weight, feel sick, or have a hangover?

Now look at some of the healthy lifelines you have used in the past that did work for you.

- Do you still use them? If not, write why not?
- Write how you might reintroduce them into your life.

*Identify and write about your stress lifelines.*

_____

_____

_____

_____

_____

_____

_____

_____

_____

_____

_____

_____

_____

_____

Is there a hobby that you have never done but have always wanted to do?

- In your journal, make an entry about that hobby. Write down how it feels to do it.
- How satisfactory is it? Is it changing your life? What do you need to learn or acquire to do the hobby?
- Write a list of stress lifelines that you have never used but want to try.

Where do you get these? By listening to friends. What have you noticed that they do when stressed? How might that change your life?

# Wrapup

In this chapter you discovered:

- How stress can make you sick
- How stress can force your body to say no
- How you can make the choice to master the stress in your life
- How to apply a couple of stress busters
- How to acquire some stress lifelines

*Don't forget to write in your journal.* The more you write, the more you know about what stresses you and what works best to handle your own stress.

# Way Four:

# Engage in Healing Emotions

## Your emotional life

**Did you know that emotions add the color** to your life and that the right emotions can help you heal? In this chapter you will discover:

- The value of your emotions
- To heal, you must feel
- How to use your toolkit of emotions
- How your writing can fine-tune your connection to your emotions

The Merriam-Webster dictionary defines an *emotion* as a noun that is:

- An affective aspect of consciousness
- A state of feeling
- A psychic and physical reaction (as anger or fear) subjectively experienced as strong feeling and

physiologically involving changes that prepare the body for immediate vigorous action

Of interest, the word emotion derives from a French word, *emouvoi,* which means *to stir up,* and the Latin word, *emovere,* which means to remove, or displace. This interesting combination of words reflects the reality that, depending on which emotion you are experiencing, you can be emotionally stimulated into action or withdrawal.

# The value of your emotions

As Dr. Jeanne Segal writes in her book, *Raising your Emotional Intelligence—Emotions Matter:* Emotions are your lifelines to self-awareness and self-preservation that deeply connect you to yourself and others, the universe, and nature.

When you first got out of your abusive relationship and moved from being a victim to being a survivor, your life was filled with changes, each one costing you some adaptation energy.

In addition, you had multiple emotions that reflected the trauma you experienced and the shock of sudden life change. So much going on at the same time sets the stage for being emotionally overwhelmed.

## Have you chosen numbness?

To cope with the emotional overload, you may have chosen to become numb, avoiding all emotions. At the time of your biggest life changes, this may have been healthy, buying you necessary breathing space.

The problem is that avoidance takes its toll if it goes on too long. What was initially a healthy defense is now a toll-taking, energy-draining vice.

Avoidance and numbness tie up your coping points and drain your vitality and energy. Your world grays out. The vibrancy of life escapes you. You are left with just pushing yourself through the steps of daily living.

What kind of life is that? A life of stumbling along among the living dead?

## Finding healthy emotions

There is a cure for numbness and avoidance: You can "medicate" yourself with the healthy emotions of life. Remember, your emotions have great value. Doni Tamblyn, author of *Laugh and Learn*, writes what your emotions can do for you:

- Help you learn information faster.
- Help you recall information better.
- Make information feel "real" for you (you tend to believe what you feel).
- Help you make better quality decisions about information (because emotions help you integrate your logic with your values).

Work to emotionally engage and you will soon have a spring back in your step and a smile back on your face and in your soul.

# To heal, you must feel

To live, you must feel. When you begin to feel, you reconnect with yourself, you become whole again. You begin to heal. Emotions are the color and spice of life.

In the past 25 years or so, Western physicians, biologists, and psychologists have begun to understand the interrelationship between our emotional states and our mental and physical well-being. This connection is not new.

The world's wisdom literature and our grandmothers have known about the mind-body connection and emotional awareness for years. What is new is scientific awareness and, therefore, the blessing which makes it "real" to the scientists and clinicians of today.

Remember what Dr. Segal said in the last section? Emotions matter! Dr. Segal proposes that emotion and intellect are but two halves of a whole, working together synergistically.

Intellect is measured by a rating known as your intelligence quotient. Dr. Segal rates the "emotional intelligence of the heart" as your EQ. Your EQ is responsible for your self-esteem, self-awareness and social adaptability. It provides you with a critical edge in many areas of your life: work, social, family, romance, and spiritual.

When you have a high EQ, you can experience feelings when they occur. Best of all, you get to truly know yourself.

To learn more about enhancing your EQ, read Dr. Segal's book, *Raising Your Emotional Intelligence.*

## Find your way

Many times when emotions are elusive and life has lost its vibrancy, it is because we have lost our way. The good news is that the very trauma you went through as a victim can now provide the stimulus to find your personal way.

Researchers working with cancer patients find that some patients use the crisis of the cancer to recover their purpose in life as well as their human character. When this happens, their crisis becomes not a personal disaster, but the greatest gift of all—they discover that life is not just about surviving.

Successful living is about learning from the great challenges of life and getting the best quality of life possible during your current lifetime.

Studying how patients with cancer find hope and mobilize to fight the cancer and survive, researchers found that one patient with a very good outcome went through distinct stages. She engaged in:

- Finding the purpose of life and hidden resources
- Confronting denial
- Taking responsibility for being ill
- Still fighting, even when going through severe existential crisis with no will to live
- Integrating her many repressed feelings and negative decisions, thus rehabilitating her character
- Confronting lack of intimacy and trust in others, thus rehabilitating the ability to love
- Rehabilitating the will to live, breaking through and falling in love
- Assuming responsibility for social relations in her life

Note that this whole process requires courage and persistence. So it is when coming to grips with major trauma and putting your life back together. It's a tough journey.

## Emotions can hold you back

Emotions such as these will hold you back if you don't acknowledge the feelings — and then manage them:

- Anger
- Holding a grudge
- Hating and envying others
- Feeling sorry for yourself

Recent research has shown that the negative emotions, such as anger, hostility, rage, and depression, decrease your immune system's functioning and seem to play a role in heart disease and early mortality. But the healing emotions will carry you through and put a little fun and meaning back into your life, all at the same time.

# How to use your toolkit of emotions

Regardless of what emotion you encounter, it is always best to address the emotion. As author Doni Tamblyn writes, "…emotions are much like teenagers. When met with intolerance, they become withdrawn and sullen. Given acceptance, they are more open and authentic…"

Her comparison doesn't stop there. She also notes that "at least emotions don't raid your refrigerator or put their feet on your furniture."

## Negative emotions

Before moving on to emotional management aimed at invoking healthy emotions, let's take a minute to talk about how to manage the emotions that are currently wreaking havoc in your life.

You already know which emotions these are, because such emotions:

- Make you feel bad.
- Cause you to engage in unhealthy behaviors such as smoking, substance or medication abuse, overeating, or excess alcohol intake, just to name a few.
- Result in your poor or compromised health status (we now know that depression causes cardiovascular disease and osteoporosis in some).

If you suffer from such emotions, consider joining Emotions Anonymous. You can learn more about them by reading their materials at Emotions Anonymous. Their website contains the following information about their 12-step approach:

> "Our program has been known to work miracles in the lives of many who suffer from problems as diverse as depression, anger, broken or strained relationships, grief, anxiety, low self-esteem, panic, abnormal fears, resentment, jealousy, guilt, despair, fatigue, tension, boredom, loneliness, withdrawal, obsessive and negative thinking, worry, compulsive behavior, and a variety of other emotional issues."

In addition to learning about handling your negative emotions, participation in groups such as Emotions Anonymous also helps you build a sense of community. *Building community is one of the Ways of a victor.*

## Humor is health

Life is too important to be taken seriously.

— *Oscar Wilde, poet and playwright*

A clown is like an aspirin, only he works twice as fast.

— *Groucho Marx, comedian*

The healing power of humor has been well documented in various places. In fact, a Google search for "humor and health" toward the end of December 2004 found over *14 million* websites addressing the issue.

Specifically, laughter lowers the stress hormones, such as epinephrine and cortisol, blood pressure, and pain. Laughing out loud can increase your energy as well as give you a way to "let go" of anger and anxiety.

# Jean's story

Author Norman Cousins first made us aware of how pain can be successfully diminished through laughing. In May of 2004, a *Calgary Herald* writer reported a similar case study:

> "For seven years, Jean Munro took morphine for her lupus pain. Now, she just laughs it off. Every morning, and as needed throughout the day, she giggles up a big belly-laugh that lasts three to five minutes.
>
> 'I have not had a pain pill for over a year now, and I'm sure it's because of the laughter,' she says."

Jean engaged in Laughter Therapy, a therapeutic approach that:

- Relaxes muscles
- Stimulates blood circulation
- Strengthens the immune system
- Exercises the heart
- Reduces the level of stress hormones
- Improves lung capacity
- Massages internal organs
- Increases the level of endorphins

### Try it out

You, too, can do laugh therapy. Try this out with some friends — one will do, and two or more are better.

- Assemble the group and then announce a five-minute laugh-out-loud session.
- Start laughing!
- At first the laughter will seem forced. Don't worry. Just keep laughing.
- Then mix it up: giggle, chortle, and imitate outrageous laughs that you have heard in the past.

As you do this and the group joins in, you will find at some point that the laughter becomes real. At some sessions, at least one person will begin to experience tears of laughter, bumping up the sense of merriment for the whole group.

### Tell yourself your favorite joke

If you are by yourself, you can kick off a five-minute laugh session by telling a joke that always makes you laugh so much that you have trouble telling the whole joke.

Here is my favorite such joke. I call it "Speed Limits."

# Speed Limits

A state trooper comes across a car that is very steadily driving along the freeway at 15 miles per hour. Other cars, coming upon this one, are slamming on their brakes and swerving to avoid hitting the slow-moving vehicle.

The trooper flashes his lights and signals the car to stop. When it pulls over, he walks up to it to discover that the auto is filled with nuns, driven by a serene Mother Superior.

"Is there trouble, officer?" the driver asks sweetly.

"Yes, Ma'am," he says. "You're driving way too slow to be on a freeway."

"But I was driving at the speed limit." She replies, pointing to the sign that says *I-15.*

"Oh," says the trooper, "that's not the speed limit. That's the number of the highway."

As the officer says this, he notices that all the other nuns in the car are blanched white as a sheet and trembling and wide-eyed.

"What's wrong with them?" he asks.

"Oh!" says the nun in the driver's seat, "we just got off Highway 121!"

I love to tell jokes, but this is one I cannot successfully tell to others, because it cracks me up to the point that I break down into the giggles before I can get all the words out. Usually, I laugh so hard that I have tears of laughter by the time I spew out the last few words.

I always get laughs when I tell the joke, but the laughs are aimed at me for not being able to get through the whole story.

### Do you have such a joke?

- Tell it right now and see if you can launch yourself into a five-minute solo laugh session.

### *My favorite joke or humorous story*

_____

_____

_____

_____

_____

_____

_____

_____

_____

_____

_____

_____

_____

# Spirituality, emotions, and your health

Many major religions and spiritual traditions embrace emotions such as compassion, love, forgiveness, and caring to achieve a state of profound happiness or joy.

 Research on religious observance, spirituality, and health status is growing. For example, religious activity (say, attendance at services) has been associated with lower blood pressure and better immune function.

Religious observance has been shown to influence life satisfaction and depression through giving meaning to life. Spiritual experiences of self-transcendence have been correlated inversely with depression and mental distress — when spiritual experiences go up, the bad emotions go down.

## Tears are good

To cry and cry and cry over the past is an exercise in futility laced with the danger of becoming trapped in our own anger or past regrets. You may already know this instinctively, and so you may try to avoid crying.

However, as anyone who has ever had a "good cry" can attest, tears can be beneficial. As French poet Voltaire wrote, "Tears are the silent language of grief."

It is good to let tears flow when grief needs to be expressed. Expressing grief and then accepting it and thanking it as an honorable emotion helps you engage and heal. Chinese folk wisdom cautions us that swallowed tears lead to ulcers.

> Tears are the safety valve of the heart when too much pressure is laid on it.
>
> — *Albert Smith*

> Tears are the summer showers to the soul.
>
> — *Alfred Austin*

 ### *Remember your tears*

Do you remember the last time you cried?

- In your journal, write a heading that describes the event or situation that caused you to cry.
- Then, below that, start free-writing. What emotions stimulated your tears? Anger, fear, loneliness, or sorrow?
- If a very wise ancient or angel were to come and sit beside you now, what would that being say to you? In your mind's eye see the person and on the page write the counsel you receive.

*This caused me to cry.*

_____

_____

_____

_____

_____

_____

_____

*What emotions were associated with the tears: anger, fear, loneliness, or sorrow?*

_____

_____

_____

_____

_____

_____

_____

_____

_____

_____

_____

_____

_____

_____

_____

_____

_____

_____

_____

_____

_____

_____

*If a very wise ancient or angel were to come and sit beside you now, what counsel would you receive? Listen and write as though the counsel is channeled to you through the universe.*

_____

_____

_____

_____

_____

_____

_____

_____

_____

_____

_____

_____

_____

_____

_____

_____

# Fine-tune your connection to your emotions

> You don't get ulcers from what you eat. You get them from what's eating you.
>
> — *Vicki Baum, novelist and playwright*

Above all, you need to know that all emotions are important. They communicate with you. When you suppress them or when you go so numb that your emotions are hidden from you, that's trouble in the making.

That's because your emotions serve you by being your very own biofeedback machine. Your emotions tell you how well (or poorly) you are doing from a psychological standpoint.

Journal writing is a form of reflection, meditation, and even prayer. It helps you to "listen within" to identify and connect with your emotional life. The reflection helps you to identify with what is really important to you.

Realizing what is ultimately important to you helps you to identify your priorities and take action.

## Some inspiration for journal writing

Here is a poem that sometimes goes by the title, "Thank you" or "Inspirations." Both titles are appropriate.

*Inspirations*

To those of you who have pushed me,
thank you. Without you I wouldn't have fallen.

To those of you who laughed at me,
thank you. Without you I wouldn't have cried.

To those of you who just couldn't love me, thank you.
Without you I wouldn't have known real love.

To those of you who hurt my feelings, thank you.
Without you I wouldn't have felt them.

To those of you who left me lonely, thank you.
Without you I wouldn't have discovered myself.

But it is to those of you who thought I couldn't do it:
It is you I thank the most. Because without you,
I wouldn't have tried.

— *Author Unknown*

### Address the emotions in the poem

- Think about each of the statements in the poem above.

- Set aside a 20-minute journal-writing session to address the emotions stimulated by each statement in the poem. Your reward will be discovering strengths that you didn't know you had.

- Write. Write. Write.

*To those of you who have pushed me, thank you. Without you I wouldn't have fallen.*

_____

_____

_____

_____

_____

_____

*To those of you who laughed at me, thank you. Without you I wouldn't have cried.*

_____

_____

_____

_____

_____

*To those of you who just couldn't love me, thank you. Without you I wouldn't have known real love.*

_____

_____

_____

_____

_____

_____

*To those of you who hurt my feelings, thank you. Without you I wouldn't have felt them.*

_____

_____

_____

_____

_____

_____

_____

_____

_____

---
 

---

*To those of you who left me lonely, thank you. Without you I wouldn't have discovered myself.*

 

---
 

---
 

---
 

---
 

---
 

---

*But it is to those of you who thought I couldn't do it: It is you I thank the most. Because without you, I wouldn't have tried.*

 

---
 

---
 

---
 

---
 

---
 

---
 

---
 

---

# Wrapup

In this chapter you discovered:

- The value of your emotions
- To heal, you must feel
- How to use our toolkit of emotions
- How your writing can fine-tune your connection to your emotions

# Way Five:

# Do What You Can With What You Have

## Anna's story

**Before Anna was arrested** for murdering her husband, Hank, in self-defense, she had a good job as a nurse at a nearby hospital. That all changed when Hank charged her in anger late one evening. The children were in bed when Hank began to accuse Anna of having an affair at work.

Just that day, Anna had bought a handgun because she was becoming more and more afraid of her husband. That night when Hank ran at her, she found the gun and pointed it at him. He stopped, looked at her and then laughed.

"Go ahead," he said. "You don't have the guts to pull that trigger." Then he lunged at her.

There was no thinking on Anna's part. She never even heard the gunshot. Suddenly Hank was staggering out the door. He collapsed and died on the porch while Anna called 911.

As with so many women in similar situations back in the 1980s, Anna was sentenced to prison for murdering Hank. Her in-laws won custody of her children and Anna was sent away to serve time. In many ways, she was fortunate. She was sentenced to only three years.

When Anna got out of prison, she had nothing. She was not allowed to see her children and she could not find work. In addition, her nursing license had been suspended. She was adrift. Soon an old college friend recommended that she start journaling.

Anna did start writing in a journal, and like so many before her, she began to feel better, and her sense of helplessness began to diminish. Outside of the writing, however, she remained unfocused and at a loss about what to do. It finally occurred to her that writing might be able to help her get some focus and order in her life.

In this chapter you will discover how you, too, can become like Anna. You will learn:

- How to determine what you want: mission, focus, and organization
- How to find your voice

## How to determine what you want: mission, focus, and organization

When Anna started journaling, she began to make lists:

- To-do lists
- Wish lists
- Lists of questions she wanted answered about her future
- Lists of new occupations she might undertake
- Lists of her favorite activities
- A list of her household belongings

On and on it went. Then Anna made a list of what she could do to help other people not go through what she had gone through. A friend put her in touch with a local shelter where she began to volunteer.

One day the director of the shelter asked her if she would speak at one of their functions and tell her story. Like many people, Anna was terrified of public speaking. But she knew this was important and volunteered to speak. She joined Toastmasters International and explained her plight and began to learn the basics of public speaking.

When the big day finally came, Anna delivered her speech to resounding applause. The director asked if she would do more presentations for them.

One day it dawned on Anna that maybe she could become a professional speaker. Back to her journal she went, making lists of pros and cons for this endeavor. She made lists of what she would need to learn about speaking for a living. She made lists of books to read and courses to take. She even made lists of what materials and help she would need to start a speaking business.

 *What is my mission? And what focus and organization do I need to find and accomplish my mission?*

_____

_____

_____

_____

_____

_____

_____

_____

# How to find your voice

### Use your writing to find your voice

Stephen R. Covey's recent book, *The 8th Habit,* addresses the need to find your own voice. When you do find your voice, you fulfill your soul's yearning for meaning and greatness. Your voice is that unique and significant essence of *you* and your significance in the universe. That uniquely *you* voice lies in the center of four arenas:

- Your talent (the natural gifts and strengths you possess)
- Your passion (those things that energize and inspire you)
- Your conscience (your small, still voice that tells you what is right)
- Need (What do others need enough to pay you to do it?)

## *Use your journal*

Use your journal to make lists.

*Write about your talents, your passions, and your conscience.*

*Write about a need in the universe that you can fill and have the passion to feel.*

_____

_____

_____

_____

_____

_____

_____

_____

_____

_____

_____

_____

_____

_____

_____

_____

_____

_____

_____

_____

## Write to find your voice

When you find your voice, your mission becomes clear. To accomplish your mission, you will need focus and organization in your life. List-making can help in both arenas.

### *Make a master list*

Now you need your master list written out.

*Make a long list of all that you need to do to accomplish what you want to accomplish.*

_____

_____

_____

_____

_____

_____

_____

_____

_____

_____

_____

_____

_____

_____

_____

_____

_____

_____

_____

_____

_____

From the master list, you will decide what you need to do over the course of the next month, and you will write down what should be accomplished over that period of time.

- Write down what you want to have completed at the end of the next month.
- At the beginning of each day, extract *no more than seven items* from your weekly "To Do" list.

Why limit yourself to seven items? If you write down more than seven things, you set yourself up with being overwhelmed by everything you need to do. Focus on one thing at a time and give that your full attention.

It is quite okay to have some personal items on the list. After all, children need to be picked up from school, groceries must be bought, and hair appointments kept. Each of those takes time.

# Determine what you have

You are richer than you think. First, let's determine how rich you are with several personal mind-storming sessions.

### *Mind-storming*

- Pull out your journal and at the top of a blank page, write: "What assets do I have?"
- Then quickly write at least 25 answers. Don't think. Don't judge. Just write.
- No answer is too big, too small, or too off-topic.

*What assets do I have?*

_____

_____

_____

_____

_____

_____

_____

_____

_____

_____

---
---
---
---
---
---
---
---
---
---

Thinking out of the box might well lead you to an "aha!" answer.

Remember Nora, earlier in the book? When she later found herself in a bit of a financial jam, she addressed the same question, "How rich am I?" Some of her answers were:

- A gasping checking account
- A dying savings account
- A getting-too-big journal
- Two cats who sleep all the time
- One cat who spends all his time prowling about on the kitchen counter
- A collection of Grandmother's recipes
- A computer
- Computer skills for using MS Word well
- A house with a big mortgage
- A digital camera

- A sense of humor (on most days)
- A small treasure chest from childhood containing my Girl Scout badges, a few dolls, and pictures of my first lemonade stand,
- My love of cooking
- Unfulfilled dreams of being a writer
- Way too much time on my hands
- Total bewilderment about what to do

As you can see, Nora's first answers were concrete. Then, as she wrote on, the answers became more abstract and scattered. When Nora went back and reviewed her answers, she found herself making connections that she would not have made before doing this exercise.

She knew she had to get work, but no one was hiring in her area. It then occurred to her that she could use the time to become her own boss and do what she had always wanted to do: write.

Back to the journal Nora went to address another question, "Given these resources, what can I do with writing?" This time, she had lots of answers, but none that seemed to address her current situation. She rewrote the question to be:

> "What can I do with what I have, right here and right now?"

More answers came and then something gelled. She immediately started on a project that eventually became an e-book: *MacCat's in the Kitchen and I'm at the Stove.* The subtitle said it all: *A Collection of Grannie's Wisdom and Cat-Safe Recipes.*

She stopped being annoyed with MacCat, the kitchen cat, and

instead began following his adventures with her digital camera. These were combined with Grannie's recipes and stories from her childhood.

The whole project took on an aura of fun and excitement that displaced Nora's distress of loss, and brought to the forefront the love and giggles she remembered from Grannie's warm kitchen. Life began to have a sense of meaning.

## Wrapup

In this chapter you discovered:

- How to determine what you want: mission, focus, and organization
- How to find your voice

# Where to go from here…

I hope this book has helped you begin
your journey back to good health and a
feeling of well-being and that it has set you
on a life path you can truly enjoy.

Remember to visit my website from time
to time:

**www.healthaftertrauma.com**

You'll find my email address on the website. I hope you'll write
to let me know how you're doing, provide any suggestions you
have for improving the book, or share someone's success story
(your own, perhaps) with others.

Also remember: *Keep writing!*

# Notes